Make a New Friend in Jesus

PassAlong Arch® Books help you share Jesus with friends close to you and with children all around the world!

When you've enjoyed this story, pass it along to a friend.   When your friend is finished, mail this book to the address below. Concordia Gospel Outreach promises to deliver your book to a boy or girl somewhere in the world to help him or her learn about Jesus.

Myself

My name _____

My address _____

_____

My PassAlong Friend

My name _____

My address _____

_____

When you're ready to give your PassAlong Arch® Book to a new friend who doesn't know about Jesus, mail it to

Concordia Gospel Outreach
3547 Indiana Avenue
St. Louis, MO 63118

PassAlong Series

God's Good Creation
Noah's Floating Zoo
Baby Moses' River Ride
Jonah's Fishy Adventure
Baby Jesus, Prince of Peace
Jesus Stills the Storm
Jesus' Big Picnic
God's Easter Plan

Copyright © 1994 Concordia Publishing House
3558 S. Jefferson Avenue, St. Louis, MO 63118-3968
Manufactured in the United States of America

1 2 3 4 5 6 7 8 9 10   03 02 01 00 99 98 97 96 95 94

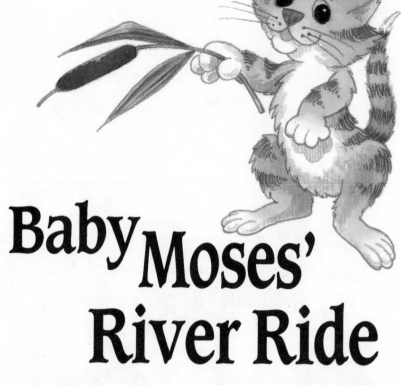

Baby Moses' River Ride

Exodus 1:1–2:10 for Children

Carol Greene
Illustrated by Michelle Dorenkamp

SAINT LOUIS

ong ago in Egypt by the River Nile,
God's people lived for quite a while.
The Hebrew people prospered and their
    numbers grew.
Then along came a pharaoh, brash
    and new.

"A pharaoh
is like a king."

By my crown and scepter, they are
    everywhere—
God's people here, God's people there!
If they join our enemies, we're in a mess.
I'd like it more if they were less."

So that evil pharaoh hatched himself a plot.
"I'll take away all that they've got.
Day and night they'll labor and they'll
    never stop.
They'll work for me until they drop."

"What a meanie!"

How the Hebrews labored—why, they
worked like slaves!
The sweat poured off of them in waves.
They built a city, Pithom. They built
Rameses too.
And still their numbers grew and grew.

Pharaoh bit his fingernails. He chewed
his thumb.
"Those women who help babies come—
From now on I want them to kill
every boy.
The girls can live. The boys destroy."

But the women didn't. All they did was fuss.
"Those babies come too fast for us.
By the time we get there, they're
already born,"
The women told him, all forlorn.

What the women said was not the least
bit true.
They lied because they wanted to
Save the Hebrew babies and they did it, so
The numbers still could grow and grow.

"What good clever women!"

Pharaoh raved and ranted till his
face turned blue.
He told his people, "I want you
To find those baby boys and when you do,
to throw
Them in the river. Hurry! Go!"

What a dreadful order!
What a dreadful plan!
That pharaoh was a dreadful man.
Throughout all of Egyptland the bad
news flew.
God's poor folk, what will you do?

"You are
a dreadful
person!"

Then a Hebrew woman had a little boy.
And what a mix of fear and joy
She felt each time she looked at him, her
baby son.
"My child, your life has just begun.

"And Pharaoh wants to end it. Well, he
won't, I say!
I'll hide my little boy away.
Quiet now, my baby. You must never cry."
And so three months crept slowly by.

"Shhhh!"

But babies will be babies.

     They just can't stay still.

And so the woman thought until

Her brain ran 'round in circles.

     Then one sunny day,

It seemed to her God showed the way.

"Look, my little baby. Here's your
     basket-boat.

I've coated it so it will float.

You're too big and noisy now for me
     to hide,

And so, dear child, you must go outside."

"I told him to be quiet."

Down along the riverbank she took
the child,
And where the reeds grew thick and wild,
She put the little basket-boat and
said a prayer.
"Dear God, please guard my baby there."

She told her daughter Miriam to
stand nearby.
"Make sure he's safe and warm and dry.
Watch and see what happens and then
let me know."
"I'll do it, Mother. You can go."

"Watch carefully, Miriam."

Baby in a basket on the River Nile,
Home of hungry crocodile,
Baby in a basket on the waters blue,
Oh, baby boy, what will you do?

Baby in a basket, hush. Now don't you cry.
Miriam is standing by.
Baby in a basket, she is watching you.
And God is watching, guarding too.

"CROCODILE!"

All at once young Miriam heard
clink, clink, clank.
And there along the riverbank,
Pharaoh's daughter wandered
in her jewels so fine,
Her maids behind her in a line.

"A bath is what I want," she said.
"Why, what is that?
An animal? A bird? A hat?
Look! It is a basket. I must see," she cried.
"Fetch it. Let me look inside."

"Be careful
with that
basket!"

Oh, it is a baby! It's a Hebrew boy,
The sort my father would destroy.
Well, he won't get this one.
    It belongs to me.
But who will nurse it? Let me see . . ."

"I'll find a nurse," said Miriam,
    "if that's your will,
A Hebrew nurse to raise him till
He's older, noble princess."
    And the princess said,
"Yes, do. His crying hurts my head."

"Now what's that Miriam up to?"

Baby in a basket, set your fears to rest.
Your nurse will be the very best.
Here comes sister Miriam and at the rear,
Your mother, smiling ear to ear.

"She will do," the princess said,
    her head inclined.
"She looks strong and wise and kind.
Take the child away now. He is wet
    and loud.
I'll pay you well." The mother bowed.

"Clever,
    clever
        Miriam!"

So his mother had her little boy again.
   She held him tight and kissed him, then
   Did the many loving things that mothers do
   And watched him closely as he grew.

Then when he was old enough,
      he had to go
Back to the princess. "Child, I know
She will treat you well, but still
      my daily prayer
Is that God watch over you,
      guard you there."

"God will!"

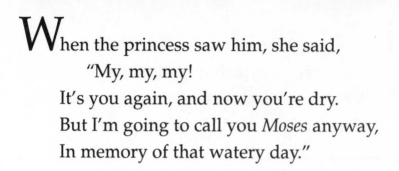

When the princess saw him, she said,
"My, my, my!
It's you again, and now you're dry.
But I'm going to call you *Moses* anyway,
In memory of that watery day."

Little Moses stayed with her till
he was grown.
But sometimes when he was alone,
That baby in a basket must have
wondered too,
What God might someday have him do.

"Moses means drawn out of the water.

I'll be right back."

Long ago in Egypt by the River Nile
God saved a little boy, and while
A baby in a basket may not sound like you,
Your God is guarding, saving too.

"Surprise!"